$16.95

Horses and Ponies

Horse and Pony Breeds

Marion Curry

GARETH**STEVENS**
GS
PUBLISHING
A Member of the WRC Media Family of Companies

Please visit our Web site at: www.garethstevens.com
For a free color catalog describing Gareth Stevens Publishing's
list of high-quality books and multimedia programs, call 1-800-542-2595 (USA)
or 1-800-387-3178 (Canada). Gareth Stevens Publishing's fax: (414) 332-3567.

Library of Congress Cataloging-in-Publication Data

Curry, Marion, 1954-
  Horse and pony breeds / by Marion Curry. — North American ed.
      p. cm. — (Horses and ponies)
    Includes bibliographical references and index.
    ISBN-10: 0-8368-6832-3 — ISBN-13: 978-0-8368-6832-6 (lib. bdg.)
    1. Horse breeds—Juvenile literature.   2. Ponies—Juvenile literature.   I. Title.
  SF291.C97   2007
  636.1—dc22   2006002855

This North American edition first published in 2007 by
Gareth Stevens Publishing
A Member of the WRC Media Family of Companies
330 West Olive Street, Suite 100
Milwaukee, WI 53212 USA

This U.S. edition copyright © 2007 by Gareth Stevens, Inc.
Original edition copyright © 2004 by Miles Kelly Publishing.
First published in 2004 by Miles Kelly Publishing Ltd., Bardfield Centre,
Great Bardfield, Essex, U.K., CM7 4SL.

Gareth Stevens managing editor: Valerie J. Weber
Gareth Stevens editor: Leifa Butrick
Gareth Stevens art director: Tammy West
Gareth Stevens designer: Kami M. Strunsee
Gareth Stevens production: Jessica Morris

Picture credits: Cover: Miles Kelly Archives; pp. 4, 8, 16, 21 © Bob Langrish; pp. 6, 13, 22 Acquire Image Media;
p. 24 (Evergreen Hamlet) Nicholas Pound; p. 25 (Moorcorner Minstrel II) Nicholas Pound. All other images
from Miles Kelly Archives, Corel, digitalvision, DigitalSTOCK, and PhotoDisc.

Printed in the United States of America

1 2 3 4 5 6 7 8 9 10 09 08 07 06

★ Cover Caption ★

This Appaloosa colt has a coat with a blanket pattern. The adult Appaloosa has a leopard coat.

Table of Contents

Words that appear in the glossary are printed in
boldface type the first time they appear in the text.

Akhal-Teke Horses

★ The Akhal-Teke is an ancient **breed** of horse, more than three thousand years old.

★ The breed began on the Turkoman Steppes in central Asia. The horse gets its name from a **nomadic** tribe known as Teke. These people lived at the Akhal oasis, a green place with water in a desert.

Akhal-Teke horses come in many colors, as the picture of this herd shows.

- People measure a horse from the ground to the top of its shoulder. The unit of measurement is called a **hand**. One hand equals 4 inches (10 centimeters), about as wide as an adult's palm and thumb.

- The average Akhal-Teke stands between 14.2 and 15.2 **hands** high, or between 4 feet 8 inches and 5 feet (1.4 to 1.5 meters) tall.

- An Akhal-Teke may be **dun**, **bay**, **chestnut**, gray, or black, with a short, silky tail. Its coat often shines like gold, silver, or copper.

- The head of an Akhal-Teke is small , and the horse has lovely, large eyes. It has one of the most beautiful bodies of all horses.

- The Akhal-Teke is famous for its **endurance.** The breed was developed to suit desert conditions. It can stand extreme heat, dry cold, and **drought**. Unlike most horses, it can live happily where grass is not available. It prefers high-protein grain and fat.

- All horses are warm-blooded mammals. Their **personalities**, however, fall into three categories: **hot-blooded**, **warm-blooded**, or **cold-blooded**. The Akhal-Teke is a hot-blooded horse, which means it tends to get excited or nervous in new situations or around new people. It learns quickly from gentle training, but it can be stubborn and refuse to obey if someone treats it badly.

> ★ *Fascinating Fact* ★
>
> The Akhal-Teke has been a racehorse for more than three thousand years.

Arabian Horses

★ The Arabian horse, or Arab, is the oldest **purebred** horse in the world. Its head is small, and it has large eyes. It has a slender nose and jaws.

★ The Arabian became the favorite horse of the Bedouin people — nomadic Arabs — as early as 3000 to 2500 B.C. Later, Europeans raised Arabian horses.

★ Arabians are famous for their beauty, speed, strength, and endurance. Many people **breed** Arabians with other horses so that the resulting **foal** would have some of the Arabian's fine traits.

★ Arabs usually stand 14 to 15.2 hands high.

★ Arabs are brave and smart. Like Akhal-Tekes, they are hot-blooded and need careful handling. They are loyal to kind owners.

★ The Arabian's running style is unique. The horse seems to float over the earth, covering a lot of ground with little effort.

Horse owners have used the Arabian to improve other horse breeds throughout history. An Anglo-Arab is a cross between a Thoroughbred and a purebred Arab.

* One of the earliest Arabian horses in the United States was a **stallion** named Ranger. He arrived in the 1760s. Some people think he was the father of the horse that George Washington rode.

* In 1879, Civil War General Ulysses S. Grant received two Arabian stallions from Abdul Hamid II, the sultan of Turkey. These horses, Leopard and Linden Tree, started a long line of Arabians in the United States.

* During the Crimean War (1853–1856), one Arabian horse raced 93 miles (153 kilometers) without being hurt, but its rider died from exhaustion.

★ *Fascinating Fact* ★

The Arabian has seventeen ribs — one fewer than other breeds.

When an Arabian is resting, its tail may hang down toward the ground. When the horse runs, it holds its tail high in the air.

Cleveland Bay and Hanoverian Horses

★ Cleveland Bays are the oldest breed of English horse. They are named after an area in northern England.

★ Cleveland Bays stand between 15.3 and 17 hands high. As their name suggests, they are reddish brown. They do not have **feathers** on their legs.

★ A Cleveland Bay is a warm-blooded horse — dependable, friendly, calm, and intelligent. It makes a good hunting horse and a good farm worker.

★ In the mid-eighteenth century, traveling salesmen, called "chapmen," used Cleveland Bays to carry their goods. The horses were called Chapman horses at that time.

Cleveland Bays make excellent driving horses because of their endurance and good personality.

★ Cleveland Bays are still popular carriage horses. The British soldiers in World War I (1914-1918) rode them into battle. British royalty still use them to pull their coaches.

★ The Hanoverian is another warm-blooded horse. It first came from Germany. A tall horse, it stands between 16 and 17 hands high. It is always a solid color.

★ Hanoverians have strong backs, a relaxed and even walk, and an easy **trot.** Horse owners value them for their calmness, good manners, and willingness to work.

★ Hanoverians were originally raised to be carriage horses and to carry soldiers.

★ Hanoverians excel as show horses. Their athletic bodies have made them popular in the United States for horse competitions. They have won many Olympic medals in jumping and **dressage**.

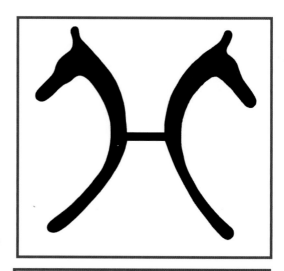

This "H" brand identifies a horse as a purebred Hanoverian.

Thoroughbred Horses

★ In **medieval** times — from the fifth to the fifteenth centuries — the English raised heavy horses that could carry a man in full armor. Arabs in the Middle East were raising lighter horses that could run fast.

★ In the seventeenth century, an Englishman brought an Arabian stallion to England and started to breed it with English **mares**. Their foals were the first of the Thoroughbreds.

★ The descendants of those horses were bred and **crossbred** to create a horse that was very fast, yet strong. Thoroughbreds are now the most famous racehorses in the world.

Thoroughbred racing is a popular sport. Races are held worldwide.

★ English kings loved racing and encouraged the development of the sport and the breeding of Thoroughbreds.

* Thoroughbreds are usually solid colors, especially bay, chestnut, or brown. Many have white markings. They stand 15 to 16.2 hands high. Their big chests hold large lungs, giving them more air to run fast. They have long, strong legs for hard running.

★ *Fascinating Fact* ★

Thoroughbreds can begin their racing career at just two years old.

---

* Beginning riders should not try to ride a Thoroughbred. This hot-blooded horse often is very excitable and difficult to control.
* The first Thoroughbred arrived in the British colonies in 1730.
* Three of the most famous Thoroughbreds in the United States were Man O' War, Citation, and Seabiscuit.
* Thoroughbreds are usually the winners of U.S. races like the Kentucky Derby and the Preakness Stakes.

The initials TB stand for Thoroughbred. The term half-bred describes a horse who has only one parent that is a Thoroughbred.

Shire and Clydesdale Horses

★ One of the largest horses in the world, the Shire, originated in England. It is a descendant of the Old English Black Horse, whose ancestors were the large horses of medieval times.

★ The Shire stands up to 18 hands high and may be bay, brown, black, or gray. It is a cold-blooded horse. The term means it is very steady, it responds well to new situations, and it follows orders easily.

★ Shires still plow the fields in some parts of Britain.

★ After World War II (1939-1945), few Shires were raised anymore, but today there is new interest in the breed.

★ Clydesdales are another breed of heavy **draft** horse.

These Shire horses are harnessed together to work. This breed has a rounded nose and large eyes set far apart.

* The breed began as Scottish farm horses more than two hundred years ago. Today owners like to decorate their manes and give them fancy harnesses.

* Clydesdales provided pulling power on farms. They also carried goods. They can pull many times more than their own weight, which is why the breed was popular for carrying goods by wagon.

* Clydesdales can grow to more than 18 hands high. They are usually bay or brown with four white legs and a mass of soft feathers on their feet. They usually have a white **blaze** on their faces.

* Horses between 15 and 16 hands high usually weigh between 700 and 1,000

The owner of this Clydesdale takes pride in his horse's healthy appearance. The horse's coat gleams, and his mane is braided with ribbons.

pounds (320 and 450 kilograms). Many Clydesdales weigh between 1,600 and 2,200 pounds (790 and 1,000 kg).

* Clydesdales may seem scary to some people because they are so big, but they are gentle and obedient.

Mustang, Paint, and Pinto Horses

★ The word *mustang* comes from a Spanish word meaning "stray" or "ownerless."

★ Spanish settlers brought Arabian and Thoroughbred horses to North America in the 1700s. Many animals broke free and formed huge herds. Both Native Americans and cowboys captured some and rode them.

★ By 1900, 2 million wild horses roamed the North American plains. Ranchers disliked the wild horses **grazing** on the same land their cattle used. They killed hundreds of thousands of mustangs.

★ By 1970, fewer than seventeen thousand mustangs still ran wild, and many citizens objected to ranchers killing them. Mustangs are now protected on government land, and U.S. citizens can adopt the horses.

★ Mustangs stand between 13 and 16 hands high and can be any color common to horses.

★ American paint horses are related to mustangs. Unlike mustangs, however, they have three defined coat patterns. These patterns are a combination of patches of white and another color. The tobiano paint has white legs and round spots. Its tail is often two colors. The overo paint has dark colored legs and bold white head markings. Its tail is one color. The tovero has coloring common to both the tobiano and overo.

★ Cowboys loved the paint horse because it worked hard.

★ Almost any breed of horse can be a pinto if it has special coloring. A pinto must have a coat with a dark background color and patches of white. It is called a piebald pinto when the darker color is black. When the background is some color other than black, it is called skewbald.

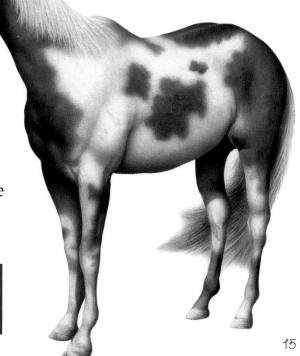

The pinto horse is a descendant of horses that came to North America with Spanish explorers.

★ The North American Indians used the pinto as a war horse because its coloring made good **camouflage**.

★ Pinto patterns probably originated from Arabian breeds. Pinto markings appear in ancient art throughout the Middle East.

Quarter Horses

★ The quarter horse got its name because it was bred to race short distances — no more than one-quarter of a mile (.4 km). It was the first breed developed in the U.S. colonies. Its **compact** body and powerful muscles made it very useful.

★ The quarter horse can be any one of thirteen colors: **sorrel**, bay, black,

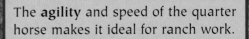

The **agility** and speed of the quarter horse makes it ideal for ranch work.

brown, buckskin, chestnut, dun, red dun, gray, **grullo**, palomino, red **roan**, and blue roan. Their only white markings are on their faces or below their knees. They measure between 14 and 16 hands high.

★ The first North American quarter horse races were held in Virginia in 1674. People bet heavily on the races, and fortunes were won and lost.

★ The quarter horse moved west with the colonists. Its speed, calm personality, and ability to handle cattle made it very helpful on ranches in the West.

★ *Fascinating Fact* ★

White Arabians are called grays. Gray quarter horses are called white. Quarter horses may be any solid color except for all white.

★ Today, quarter horses compete in rodeo events, such as roping and barrel racing. They also excel in English dressage and show jumping. They are the most popular riding horse in the United States.

★ Some quarter horses famous for racing in the United States include Wimpy, Go Man Go, Easy Jet, and Dash for Cash. Refrigerator earned more than $2 million in his racing career.

★ Another famous quarter horse is Docs Keeping Time. This stallion had an unsuccessful racing career but was the star of the movie *Black Beauty*. He also starred in the television series *The Black Stallion* and played Gulliver in *The Horse Whisperer*. In 1994, this horse won the Silver Spur Award, an Academy Award for horses.

Appaloosa Horses

★ Cave drawings in France, going back to 1800 B.C., show some spotted horses that look like Appaloosas. Egyptian tomb paintings from 1415 B.C. also show spotted horses. The artists' models may be ancient ancestors of present-day Appaloosas.

★ The Nez Perce Indians, however, were the first to choose certain horses to mate to produce a line, or breed, of spotted horse.

★ The Nez Perce lived in northwestern United States near the Palouse River in an area that is now Washington and Idaho. It was an ideal place to raise horses. The Nez Perce were excellent horsemen and became a wealthy tribe by trading their Appaloosas.

★ The breed was almost destroyed in the late 1800s when the U.S. army captured the Nez Perce Indians and killed their horses.

★ The base color of an Appaloosa's coat can be bay, black, chestnut, or palomino. They have short manes and tails and usually stand 14.2 to 16 hands high.

★ An Appaloosa's spots are often unique, but some of the patterns have names. When

> **★ Fascinating Fact ★**
>
> Most Appaloosa foals are born with light coats that eventually grow darker. Gray Appaloosas, however, start dark and become lighter.

an Appaloosa's rump is a different color from its neck and back, it is said to have a blanket coat. The blanket could be a plain color or spotted. If the Appaloosa has spots all over it, it has a leopard coat. Appaloosas often have black-and-white markings on their feet.

The foal in the picture has a spotted blanket coat. The full-grown Appaloosa has a leopard coat.

★ After almost becoming extinct, more than 500,000 Appaloosas are registered in the Appaloosa Horse Club today.

Other Horse Breeds

* The American Standardbred is the most popular **harness racer** in the world. The horses are called Standardbred because each horse has to pass a test, or meet a certain standard, to qualify as one of the breed.

* The Brabant, or Belgium Heavy Draft, is a descendant of the medieval heavy warhorse. It is the most popular draft breed in the United States. These large horses stand between 16 and 18 hands high. They are usually chestnut or roan with light manes and tails.

* The Trakehner stands between 16 and 16.2 hands high and can be any color common to horses. The breed comes from Prussia in today's Germany.

* The Percheron is a strong, heavy horse, 15 to 17 hands high. Usually gray or black, this breed began in France and is one of the strongest draft horses in the world.

* The Yili from China is a new breed, developed by breeding

Percherons have broad chests with strong legs and large feet.

Russian and Chinese horses together. They can be draft or riding horses. They stand about 14 hands high and are usually bay in color. Because of their great **stamina**, they can cover distances quickly.

★ The Canadian horse breed is famous for its stamina, gentleness, athletic ability, and willingness to please. This breed is usually black and stands 14 to 16 hands high.

★ The Dutch Warmblood comes from Holland. It is used on farms and also excels in competitions.

★ The Falabella is the best-known miniature horse breed. It is usually about 30 inches (76 centimeters) tall at the shoulder.

★ Mostly chestnut and standing over 16 hands high, the Selle Français is an all-around competition horse. Its name means "French saddle horse."

The powerful legs of the Dutch Warmblood help it jump easily over hurdles in competitions.

Shetland and Highland Ponies

★ Shetland **ponies** are native to the Shetland Islands off the coast of northern Scotland. They lived there with poor grass and bitter winds. In that climate, animals that can conserve body heat are able to stay alive. The ponies developed small, compact bodies to survive.

★ Shetland ponies are generally measured in inches or centimeters instead of hands. The Shetland is the smallest British pony, usually not more than 42 inches (107 cm) high. Miniature Shetlands are only 34 inches (87 cm) high.

★ Shetland ponies can be any color common to horses, but they are never spotted. They have a coat with two layers. In winter, guard hairs help keep out the wind and rain.

Shetland ponies once pulled carts through underground mine tunnels. Now they are popular as children's ponies.

They also have particularly thick manes and tails to help keep them warm. In summer, they develop a short, shiny coat.

★ The Shetland is the strongest of all breeds for its size. Shetlands were originally working ponies who carried seaweed and peat — clumps of dried grass and dirt for fires.

★ The Highland pony stands between 12 and 14 hands high. It comes from the Highlands of Scotland where the climate was also harsh.

★ Highland ponies come in a variety of colors, including dun, brown, bay, and black. The Highland ponies from the island of Rhum are often chestnut with a silver mane.

★ Highland ponies are famous for carrying heavy loads over very rough ground. They are extremely sure-footed on hills. Small farmers have used them for centuries. Today, they are popular horses for the disabled to ride, and they are wonderful animals to carry tents and supplies on cross-country trips.

★ Connemara ponies developed in the rugged hills of western Ireland. Hardy, agile animals, they can easily jump fences and walls.

★ Regarded as cold-blooded, Connemaras are smart and follow orders well.

★ Connemara ponies are usually gray, black, brown, or dun, but sometimes they are roan, chestnut, or palomino. They measure between 13 and 14.2 hands high.

★ Farmers used the ponies to carry heavy items, such as peat, potatoes, and seaweed, and to pull wagons holding many people. Today, these graceful, athletic animals are popular ponies for children.

The Connemara makes an excellent competition pony for teenagers or small adults.

★ Connemara ponies are often crossed with Thoroughbred or Arabian horses. The resulting crossbred horses are successful in dressage and jumping competitions.

- ★ The New Forest pony comes from southern England, where some can still be found living wild in the New Forest region. They are usually bay, brown, or gray, standing 12 to 14.2 hands high.

- ★ New Forest ponies are naturally sure-footed and hardy. A long, smooth stride makes New Forest ponies comfortable to ride, and they are ideal for long, cross-country trips.

- ★ These ponies are surprisingly fast, especially over rough roads. They are very good for harness racing and polo.

- ★ The New Forest pony adapts well to people with different riding abilities, so it is ideal for families who want a pony for adults as well as children.

A high-quality New Forest pony excels in competitions.

Haflinger and Icelandic Ponies

★ Standing between 13.1 and 14.2 hands high, the Haflinger is a palomino or chestnut pony with a light-colored mane and tail. The breed takes its name from the village of Haflinger near the border of Austria and Italy.

★ Haflingers have been bred to be friendly and easy to work with. For centuries they have served mountain farmers and herders in many ways.

★ The Haflinger is small and strong. It has large eyes, and it enjoys exercise.

★ Haflingers make good riding ponies, but they also have many other talents. They can pull carts and travel long distances. They are often used by acrobats who perform tricks on their backs. They are a popular breed at centers for disabled riders because of their calm natures.

★ The Icelandic language has no word for pony, so the Icelandic is always called a horse, even though it is less than 13.2 hands high.

★ The coats of Icelandic horses have three layers to help them withstand the harsh climate of Iceland.

★ Icelandic horses usually live a long time and are only fully grown at seven years old.

★ *Fascinating Fact* ★

The Icelandic horse is a descendant of the ancient horses brought to Iceland from Norway in the ninth century.

---

* Icelandic horses can be any color. They have a stocky build and are noted for good eyesight and a hardy nature.
* The horses have a special four-beat **gait**, called the tölt.

The tölt is so smooth that a rider can carry a full glass of liquid in one hand without spilling a drop. Any speed tölt is possible — slow and gracious or as fast as a gallop.

Haflingers are small and strong. They are a hardy breed ideally suited to working on mountain slopes.

Other Pony Breeds

★ The Przewalski horse was a wild horse discovered in Mongolia in eastern Asia in 1881. Many were captured and put in zoos, but they did not survive well there. By 1969, all the wild Przewalski horses had died out. The captive horses were then returned to a forest preserve in Mongolia.

The high-stepping walk of the Hackney makes it unsuitable as a riding pony but excellent as a driving pony.

★ The Hackney is a showy, high-stepping pony. This breed was raised specifically to pull carriages.

★ The Eriskay ponies from the island of Eriskay in the Hebrides in Great Britain are almost extinct. Machines took over their usual jobs, and people nearly stopped breeding them. Recently breeding groups have worked hard to preserve them.

★ Chincoteagues are the only pony that began in the United States. They are extremely hardy and can survive without a lot of grass. Several wild Chincoteagues still live on islands off the coast of Virginia.

★ Camargue ponies come from southern France. Many still live in wild herds on salt marshes.

★ The Vikings used the Fjord pony in battle. They are striking-looking ponies — dun colored with a stripe on their backs. Fjord ponies traditionally have their coarse manes trimmed in a crescent shape. They stand between 14 and 14.2 hands high.

★ The Konik pony is still used in rural areas throughout Poland for farm work.

★ Brittish settlers brought several pony breeds to Canada. These ponies crossbred, producing the Newfoundland pony Standing 11 to 14.2 hands high, they are usually brown with a thick mane and tail.

> ★ *Fascinating Fact* ★
>
> Camargue ponies are usually gray and are known as the "white horse of the sea."

Glossary

agility: ability to move and turn quickly

ancestors: animals or people from whom an individual or group is descended

bay: reddish brown with a dark mane

blaze: a white marking on the face

breed (noun): a group related by common ancestors

breed (verb): to produce offspring

camouflage: to hide or disguise

chestnut: reddish brown

cold-blooded: friendly, steady and able to follow orders well

compact: solid, small

crossbred: when a horse or pony of one breed is mated with a horse or pony of another breed; mixed

descendants: over a long period of time, the young of an individual or group

draft: used to pull heavy loads

dressage: an event in which a horse following orders moves precisely

drought: a long time with no rainfall

dun: grayish yellow with black mane

endurance: ability to put up with hardship

feathers: clumps of hair above the hoof

foals: horses less than one year old

gait: a manner of moving on foot

grazing: feeding on plants and grass

grullo: a silver-blue color

hand: a measurement; one hand is 4 inches (10 centimeters)

harness racer: a horse that races pulling a two-wheeled carriage

hot-blooded: excitable and nervous in new situations and around new people

mares: adult female horses

medieval: between the fifth and fifteenth centuries

nomadic: traveling from place to place

personalities: sets of qualities and behaviors

ponies: small horses, less than 14.2 hands high

purebred: an animal whose ancestors are all the same breed

roan: having a base color lightened by white hairs

sorrel: a light, bright chestnut, often with a white tail

stallion: a male horse

stamina: strength, endurance

trot: a moderately fast walk

warm-blooded: calm, intelligent, and able to learn easily

For More Information
Books

Appaloosa Zebra: A Horse Lover's Alphabet. Jessie Haas (Greenwillow Books)

The Arabian Horse. Edge Books: Horses (series). Carrie A. Braulick (Capstone Press)

Horse and Pony Breeds. DK Riding Club (series). Carolyn Henderson (Dorling Kindersley Publishing)

Horse & Pony Breeds. Kingfisher Riding Club (series). Sandy Ransford (Kingfisher)

The Horse Breeds Poster Book. Bob Langrish (Storey Publishing)

An Instant Guide to Horses. Instant Guide (series). David Burn and Cecilia Fitzsimons (Gramercy)

Where Horses Run Free: A Dream for the American Mustang. Joy Cowley and Layne Johnson (Boyds Mills Press)

Web Sites

Breeds of Livestock
www.ansi.okstate.edu/breeds/horses
Information about all kinds of horse breeds

Przewalski's Horses
www.nationalgeographic.com/kids/creature_feature/0204/horses2.html
Facts about wild horses

The Wild Horse
yahooligans.yahoo.com/content/animals/species/4066.html
Fun facts about the horses of Mongolia

Publisher's note to educators and parents: Our editors have carefully reviewed these Web sites to ensure that they are suitable for children. Many Web sites change frequently, however, and we cannot guarantee that a site's future contents will continue to meet our high standards of quality and educational value. Be advised that children should be closely supervised whenever they access the Internet.

Index